CONTENTS

Also available in this series:

Crash Course Home Recording

Crash Course Bass

Crash Course Drums

Crash Course DJ

Crash Course Electric Guitar

Printed and bound in the UK by MPG Books Ltd, Bodmin

Published in the UK by SMT, an imprint of Sanctuary Publishing Limited, Sanctuary House, 45-53 Sinclair Road, London W14 0NS, United Kingdom

www.sanctuarypublishing.com

Copyright: Paul White 2004

Cover image copyright and courtesy of Alamy

ISBN: 1-84492-078-X

CRASH COURSE MIDI

Paul White

smt

WEEK 8

INTRODUCTION

The introduction of MIDI over two decades ago enabled a huge number of musicians to create and record their own music using synthesisers, samplers, drum machines and computers. Indeed, it could be argued that MIDI – followed by the computer-based sequencer – actually helped to shape the way pop music sounds today.

MIDI is not a difficult technology to use, at least at a practical level, and books that start off with explanations of digital bits and bytes, data structure and so on rather miss the point, as most of these details are completely invisible to the user, just as the inside of your TV set remains invisible when you're switching channels, looking for something to watch.

The aim of this book is to explain the basic concept of MIDI and then to explore its practical music-making applications in as straightforward a way as possible, dividing the work into weekly sections containing practical exercises that you can try for yourself. At the end of each week is a series of questions designed to make sure you've understood the concepts.

Once you've worked your way through this course, you'll know what you can expect to achieve using MIDI, and you'll know how to go about achieving it. Then, if you want to know more about the advanced uses of MIDI, or if you're curious about what all those bits and bytes do, you'll be ready to move on to more advanced reading.

WEEK 1

INTRODUCING MIDI

The first section of *Crash Course MIDI* provides an overview of what MIDI can do for you, but without going into unnecessary technical detail. The practicalities will follow in subsequent sections, but remember that this is a Crash Course, so some of the rather more obscure or little-used aspects of MIDI will be either omitted completely or described only briefly. Where I feel it's important to be aware of something without actually needing to know too much about it in detail, I'll tag the section with an 'ADVANCED' note. Like all books in this series, *Crash Course MIDI* is split into eight weekly sections, but each section could easily be covered in one day if you're particularly keen!

> **" THE PROS SAY...**
>
> MIDI is not audio!

A LITTLE HISTORY

MIDI was developed back in the early 1980s, when the major synth developers agreed on a standard system by means of which electronic instruments from different manufacturers could be connected together in such a way that music data could be sent from one to the other. They called their idea the *musical instrument digital interface*, or MIDI for short. There are many definitive works on MIDI, but here I'm taking the need-to-know approach to help you become a MIDI *user*, which is not the same thing as being a computer *expert*. As I said earlier, this Crash Course includes a number of practical examples, which I'd encourage you to try for yourself so that you get a feel for using MIDI as soon as possible.

You don't need to concern yourself with data structure or other arcane aspects of the mechanics of MIDI, although, if you decide that you'd like to pursue that side of things further, there are many excellent books out there that will take you where the majority of users fear to tread!

WHAT DOES MIDI DO?

The first statement that should be written in flashing red letters two feet high is 'MIDI IS NOT THE SAME THING AS AUDIO!' The data that travels along your MIDI cables is more like an electrical representation of a written music score, a simple series of instruction that tells the performers (in this instance, synthesisers, samplers and drum machines) what notes to play and when to play them. However, you don't have to be able to read or write music notation to be able to use MIDI.

It's important to understand that MIDI is useful for controlling only those electronic musical instruments that have MIDI facilities built into them (which are the vast majority, these days). When used in combination with a MIDI sequencer, MIDI makes it possible for musicians working at home to create and play back multipart compositions featuring the sounds of multiple electronic instruments. Most MIDI sequencers are software based and run on either the PC Windows or Mac OS platforms, although there are hardware sequencers available for those who prefer not to use desktop computers and there are a number of keyboard synthesisers that have basic sequencing facilities built into them. Sequencers will be discussed in more detail later, but they are essentially multitrack recorders for the recording and playback of MIDI data.

MIDI

 While hardware sequencers are usually self-contained, a computer-based MIDI sequencer comprises the computer system, suitable MIDI sequencing software and a MIDI interface, which may be a separate box or part of a soundcard. This setup must be used in conjunction with one or more MIDI instruments – which may be hardware boxes, chips on a soundcard or software plugins (see Glossary) – and, of course, a MIDI keyboard or other suitable controller.

At this point, don't worry about the term *MIDI data*. I'll explain what it means after I've looked at some of the benefits that MIDI brings to the musician.

To start with, it's important to note that MIDI is mainly applicable to keyboard players, as the keyboard is the best-suited means of generating MIDI information. There are practical alternatives for guitarists, violinists, wind players, drummers and so on, but all the examples in this book will be illustrated by way of keyboard instruments.

YOUR MIDI ORCHESTRA

So what does MIDI enable you to do? At its simplest, it allows you to control (ie play) multiple instruments from a single keyboard, but by far the greatest benefit MIDI gives the user is the facility for *sequencing*. MIDI sequencing gives the solo musician the means to record all the different parts of a composition from a keyboard, one at a time, and then hear them all playing together. This sounds rather like what you can do with a multitrack tape recorder, but remember that a MIDI sequencer doesn't record sound; at its most basic, it simply records data generated when you press and release the keys on the controlling instrument and it also records how hard you play them.

Because MIDI data simply comprises electronic messages and not the sounds themselves, a separate MIDI instrument is required to play back each part of a MIDI composition. However, this isn't actually as expensive as it might sound because most modern instruments and soundcards behave as several synthesisers in one.

After recording a MIDI part into a sequencer, you can change the tempo or pitch of the recorded performances independently of each other and you can experiment with the musical arrangement by copying or moving sections of your recording to new locations within the song. If you think of sequencer editing as being similar to using a word processor to edit or reorganise text, you won't be far off the mark.

The digital MIDI information that is communicated from a sequencer to a synthesiser is analogous to that which passes from a composer to a performer via the score, except in the case of MIDI the storage medium is computer memory and disks, not a written series of dots and squiggles. Furthermore, all the instruments in the MIDI orchestra are electronic and the only performing musician is you! Well, at least that means that everyone will turn up to your recording session and no one will ask for overtime payment!

Without a sequencer, the uses of MIDI are largely limited to allowing you to do things like play one keyboard and have the sounds produced by another that's connected to your 'master' keyboard via a MIDI cable. This can be useful in live performance, as it means you don't have to move to a different keyboard every

time you need to use a different instrument, but it's of limited use in composition, where you really need a sequencer in order to make MIDI work for you. Contrary to popular belief, using MIDI doesn't make music sound mechanical; it's just a different way of recording. The musical performance element is all down to you. The advantage of recording MIDI over recording a live keyboard performance to tape is that almost everything about your MIDI performance – from tempo and pitch to the arrangement and the sounds used – can be changed at a later time. Again, this strikes a parallel to music scores, which can be refined and edited many times before the final performance.

THE MIDI KEYBOARD

The first component in any MIDI system is the MIDI keyboard. This might be a synthesiser or it might be a 'dumb' master keyboard that generates only MIDI data and has no sound capability of its own. A MIDI *instrument* (ie one with built-in sounds) can be recognised by the MIDI In, MIDI Out and MIDI Thru sockets on the back panel. A MIDI *keyboard* (often called a *controller keyboard*), on the other hand, needs only a MIDI Out socket. All but the simplest MIDI keyboards are 'velocity sensitive', which means that the harder you hit the keys, the louder the notes will sound (provided that the instrument you're controlling responds to MIDI velocity data). Most will also have a jack socket for the connection of a sustain pedal.

 If you don't have a velocity-sensitive master keyboard, all notes will play at the same level, as on an organ.

TOP TIP

If you choose to use a sequencer and a keyboard synth as your master keyboard, it's important that the keyboard has a facility called *MIDI Local Off*. Without this, using it with a sequencer will be less straightforward. I'll explain why later, but if you go shopping for a keyboard synth before finishing this book, be sure that you can switch it to Local Off mode.

BUT HOW CAN I USE MIDI?

From the user's point of view, MIDI is little more than a system of connecting cables; its inner workings can largely be ignored, in the same way that the workings of an international telephone exchange can be ignored by someone trying to phone a friend in another country.

Connecting MIDI instruments is accomplished by means of standard MIDI cables, which have five-pin DIN plugs on either end. DIN cables can be wired in different ways, however, so be sure you ask specifically for MIDI cables. The only technical detail you need to know is how long you'd like them to be!

THE PROS SAY...

Learn the basics first. You'll pick up the rest as you need it.

MIDI data is in a digital form, which you can imagine as being a kind of ultra-fast Morse code for computers. Perhaps now is the time to look a little more closely at precisely what musically useful information can be passed from one MIDI

MIDI

instrument or device to another using MIDI. I'll start with the most important concepts and then introduce new ones on a strictly need-to-know basis.

THE REAL SECRET OF MIDI

The most important elements of music are note pitches and note timings. The action of pressing a key on an electronic instrument generates an electronic message that tells the instrument's internal circuitry what note to play and how loud to play it. With a MIDI instrument or master keyboard, this information is also sent to the MIDI Out socket in the form of a note number identifying the key that was pressed, along with another number relating to how quickly the key was pressed. Why is the speed important? Well, the loudness of the note depends on how hard the key is hit, which is really the same thing as saying how fast the key is pushed down. This playing intensity is known as *velocity*.

When the key is released, a Note Off message is sent, telling the instrument when to stop playing the note. Thus a simple MIDI note message generated by pressing and releasing a key can be used to tell a remote MIDI instrument what note to play, when to play it, how loud to play it and when to stop playing it.

Up to 128 different notes can be handled by MIDI, where each key on the keyboard has its own note number. The number 128 comes up a lot in MIDI, as it's the maximum range that can be carried by any single MIDI message and is due to the way in which MIDI data is structured.

Although the pitch that the MIDI note message represents is determined by which key is pressed, it is possible to transpose MIDI data (by adding or subtracting a constant value from the note number) before it reaches its destination. For example, if you subtract two from each of the MIDI note values, the performance will be transposed down by two semitones. This is how sequencers allow you to play back your recordings at different pitches. To keep things simple, though, for now let's assume that, unless otherwise stated, pressing a key results in the corresponding note being played by the receiving device.

MIDI NOTE DATA

If the MIDI Out of the keyboard currently being played (the *master keyboard*) is plugged into the MIDI In socket of a second MIDI instrument (the *slave*), the slave is able to play the notes that are performed on the master keyboard. This is the simplest form of MIDI connection, and is shown in Figure 1.1. You can try this for yourself very shortly – after I've explained a few more simple but important points, such as what those MIDI In, Out and Thru sockets are for.

- **MIDI Out** – Sends the MIDI data from a controlling MIDI device (master) to the other MIDI devices that it is controlling (slaves), or to a MIDI sequencer. In a basic MIDI system, only the master device (keyboard) and the sequencer (where one is used) need to have their MIDI Outs connected.

- **MIDI In** – Receives MIDI information, which is acted upon by the device (if the MIDI data is intended for that device) and also passed on to the device's MIDI Thru

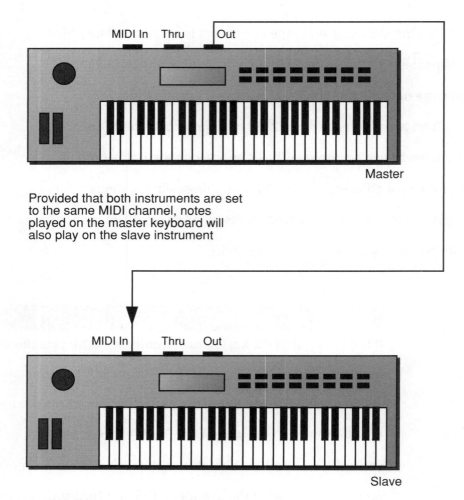

Provided that both instruments are set to the same MIDI channel, notes played on the master keyboard will also play on the slave instrument

Figure 1.1: Basic MIDI connection (master plus slave)

socket unchanged. If any of the incoming information is addressed to an instrument, it will respond to the MIDI data exactly as if it was being played directly from its own keyboard. (I'll explain the term 'addressed' in the next section.)

- **MIDI Thru** – Transmits an exact copy of the MIDI In signal, allowing several MIDI instruments to be linked together.

I'll take this opportunity to repeat what I said earlier: MIDI is not sound! It's surprising how many people listen patiently to a description of MIDI sequencing and then ask if they can record their voice or acoustic guitar over MIDI as well! There are ways of recording conventional audio into computers, and even into the audio sections of many sequencers, but this has nothing to do with MIDI.

PRACTICAL EXERCISE

We haven't quite covered all the background information we need to connect up a MIDI system yet, so first of all simply try out your MIDI keyboard (if it has a built-in synth) and examine the way its sounds respond to how hard you press the keys. Also, try the pitch-bend and modulation wheels (if fitted), as these can also be used in a MIDI system.

Locate the MIDI Setup menu for your synth and find the Local On/Off page. Note that, if you select Local Off, you won't be able to play any of the sounds in your synthesiser unless it's connected to a sequencer.

Look at the other parameters in the MIDI Setup menu and make a note of them. Don't change anything yet, though; just make sure you know how to find them for later. It's also worth checking out the rear panel of your keyboard to locate the MIDI and sustain-pedal jack sockets. Finally, set up the arrangement shown in Figure 1.1, as we'll be putting that to the test at the beginning of Week 2.

MIDI

End of the week, time for a short test to make sure you know what you think you know. Everything here was covered this week. If you can't answer any of the questions, go back and check!

1   What do the letters MIDI stand for?

2   What do you understand by the term *MIDI velocity*?

3   What MIDI message signals that a key has been pressed?

4   Name the three MIDI sockets.

5   Can MIDI be used to record voices, guitars or other audio?

THE PROS SAY...

Don't chain. Use a thru box!

WEEK 2

MORE ABOUT MIDI

OK, this might be billed as Week 2, but I'm sure you haven't spent a whole week just prodding your keyboard and checking out its MIDI menus, so treat yourself to a coffee and let's continue.

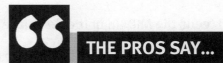

THE PROS SAY...

MIDI doesn't make bad music; people make bad music!

MIDI MODULES

If MIDI allows everything to be controlled from one master keyboard, why is it that the slave instruments need keyboards of their own? Good question, and the answer is that they don't. Instead, you can use what's known as a *MIDI sound module*, which in effect is the sound-generating and MIDI-interfacing electronic part of a keyboard instrument without the keyboard attached. This makes such devices cheaper, because they don't cost as much to build as full-sized keyboard instruments, and means that they don't take up as much room. It's also possible to control multiple modules from a single master keyboard, but if you don't want them all to play at the same time, you need to know about MIDI channels. (This is the 'addressing' business I mentioned at the end of Week 1.)

MIDI CHANNELS

MIDI channels are the means by which certain messages are sent so that they are recognised and acted upon only by the intended instruments and are ignored by all the others. Without addresses, every instrument would try to play every MIDI message presented to its MIDI In socket, which would cause chaos!

MIDI

Simple MIDI systems are linked in a *daisy-chain* manner, where the MIDI Out of
the master keyboard feeds the MIDI In of the first slave, then the MIDI Thru of the
slave feeds the MIDI In of the next slave in line, and so on. This form of linking is
simple, but it does mean that all slaves receive exactly the same MIDI
information. For the master instrument to communicate with just one specific
slave without the others playing at the same time, MIDI channels must be used.

I like to explain MIDI channels by saying that MIDI note messages are tagged with
an invisible address label carrying their MIDI channel number, and this isn't far off
the mark. Like I said, MIDI messages are acted upon only when they are received
by a MIDI instrument or device set to the same MIDI channel number as that
'written on' the address label on the MIDI note message. Other MIDI devices set to
different MIDI channels will simply ignore the MIDI message.

MIDI was conceived with 16 channels, and there's a close analogy here between
MIDI channels and television channels. Many different TV programmes reach the
TV receiver down the same length of cable, but we see only one channel at a time
in accordance with the TV channel currently selected. The main point to
understand is that all the programmes are fed into the TV set simultaneously, but
the channel system allows us to tune into them one at a time.

MIDI allows us to do much the same thing – the information sent down the MIDI
cable can be on any one of 16 channels (as selected on the master keyboard or
sequencer) while the connected instruments may each be set to receive on any

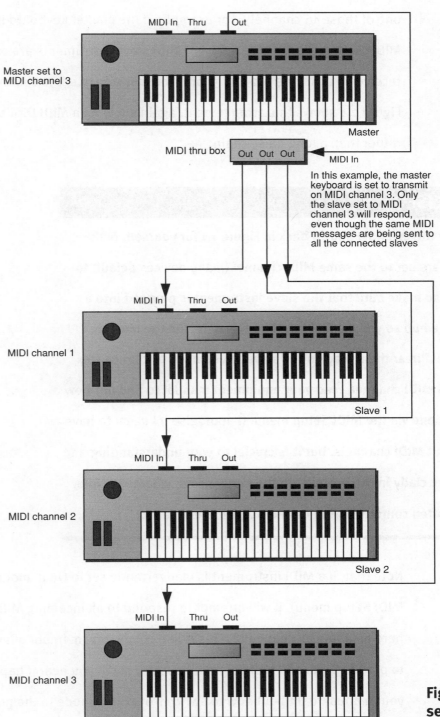

MIDI In Thru Out

Master set to
MIDI channel 3

Master

MIDI thru box   Out Out Out

MIDI In

In this example, the master
keyboard is set to transmit
on MIDI channel 3. Only
the slave set to MIDI
channel 3 will respond,
even though the same MIDI
messages are being sent to
all the connected slaves

MIDI In Thru Out

MIDI channel 1

Slave 1

MIDI In Thru Out

MIDI channel 2

Slave 2

MIDI In Thru Out

MIDI channel 3

Slave 3

**Figure 2.1: Master
sends on channel 1;
slaves receive on
channels 1, 2 or 3**

one of those 16 channels. For example, if the master keyboard is set to send on MIDI channel 3 and three different MIDI slave instruments are connected up to receive on channels 1, 2 and 3, only the instrument set to channel 3 will respond. Figure 2.1 shows this arrangement, again showing a MIDI thru box being used rather than a long daisy chain.

PRACTICAL EXERCISE

You're now ready to try the example shown back in Figure 1.1 for yourself. Make sure that both devices are set to the same MIDI channel (many devices default to MIDI channel 1), and also make sure that the slave instrument is plugged into a sound system and turned up so you can hear it. Hit a few notes on the master keyboard and you should hear them play on the slave. If you need to change the transmitted or received MIDI channel, read your equipment manual to find out how to do this. It's usually done via the MIDI Setup menu. (I apologise if I seem to have laboured the point about MIDI channels, but it is crucial to your understanding and application of MIDI, especially in the context of MIDI sequencers, where multiple slave instruments are often controlled at once and play different parts.)

Note that, if a MIDI instrument is inadvertently set to Omni mode (an option in the MIDI Setup menu), it will attempt to respond to all incoming MIDI data ('omni' here meaning all channels). This is like having one member of an orchestra trying to play all parts of a score simultaneously, and if you hear it happening, look in your manual to find out how to switch from Omni mode to the more usual Poly mode. (I'll talk more about MIDI modes a little later.)

 The majority of MIDI instruments remember what mode they are set to, even if they've been switched off and back on again, but a few older instruments default to Omni mode whenever they're switched on. In this case, you need to switch to Poly mode manually before starting work.

MORE ON CONNECTIONS

While in theory a MIDI daisy chain can be infinitely long, this turns out to be untrue in practice. What actually happens is that the MIDI signal deteriorates slightly as it passes through each instrument, and after a chain of three of four instruments the signal starts to become unreliable and notes may start getting stuck on, or even refuse to play at all.

The best solution is to use what's known as a MIDI thru box, which takes the Out from the master keyboard or sequencer and splits it into several Thru connections used to feed the individual modules directly. Figure 2.2 shows the standard method of daisy chaining, while Figure 2.3 shows the same system wired using a MIDI thru box.

Chaining MIDI Thru connectors doesn't cause timing delays; most audible MIDI delays can be attributed either to too much data being sent at once or to delays within the instruments themselves. A typical synthesiser or module takes several milliseconds to sound once a MIDI note message has been received. (Most people are unable to perceive delays of less than 15ms or so.)

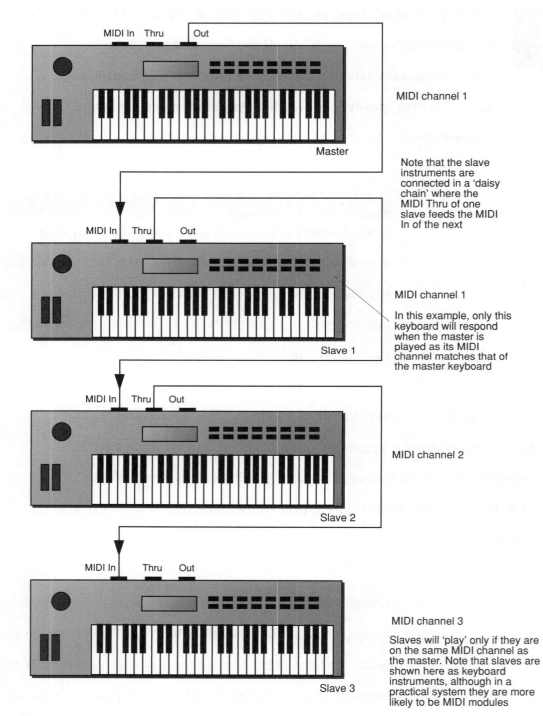

Master

MIDI channel 1

Note that the slave instruments are connected in a 'daisy chain' where the MIDI Thru of one slave feeds the MIDI In of the next

MIDI channel 1

In this example, only this keyboard will respond when the master is played as its MIDI channel matches that of the master keyboard

Slave 1

MIDI channel 2

Slave 2

MIDI channel 3

Slaves will 'play' only if they are on the same MIDI channel as the master. Note that slaves are shown here as keyboard instruments, although in a practical system they are more likely to be MIDI modules

Slave 3

Figure 2.2: Multiple slaves on different MIDI channels

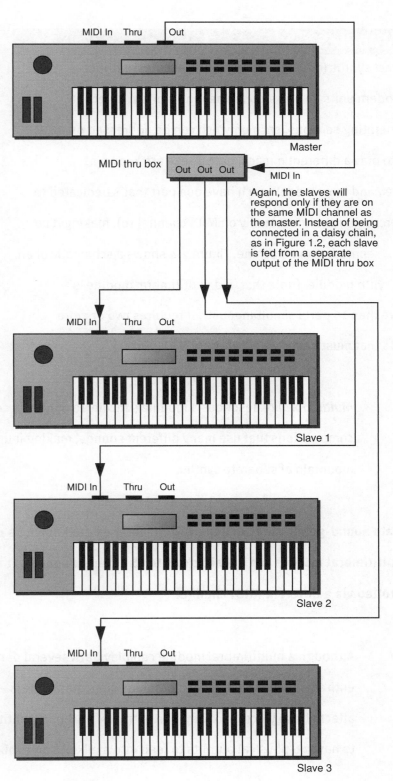

Figure 2.3: Using a MIDI thru box

Again, the slaves will respond only if they are on the same MIDI channel as the master. Instead of being connected in a daisy chain, as in Figure 1.2, each slave is fed from a separate output of the MIDI thru box

MIDI

MULTITIMBRAL MODULES

MIDI modules are in effect synths (or samplers or drum machines) without keyboards, but most modern units go one step further and contain several independent sound-generating sections, each of which can be addressed on a different MIDI channel to play a different musical part. These are known as *multitimbral instruments*, and most models each have one part that's dedicated to producing drum and percussion sounds (usually on MIDI channel 10), making it no longer essential to buy a separate drum machine. Figure 2.4 shows a schematic of an eight-part multitimbral synth module. (Note that, if a multitimbral module is designed to handle more than 16 parts simultaneously, it requires two or more independent MIDI inputs that must be fed from separate MIDI ports.)

Multitimbrality describes a module's facility to play back complex musical compositions that use many different sounds, making it unnecessary to buy a mountain of separate synths.

The separate sound-generating sections within modules are known as *parts*. A 16-part multitimbral module can play back up to 16 different sounds at once, each controlled via a different MIDI channel.

Although a multitimbral module can play back several parts, these are rarely entirely independent of each other, as some parameters – effects, particularly – can affect all the voices globally. Furthermore, a 16-part multitimbral module is unlikely to have 16 physical outputs to feed into a mixer; some mixing is usually done

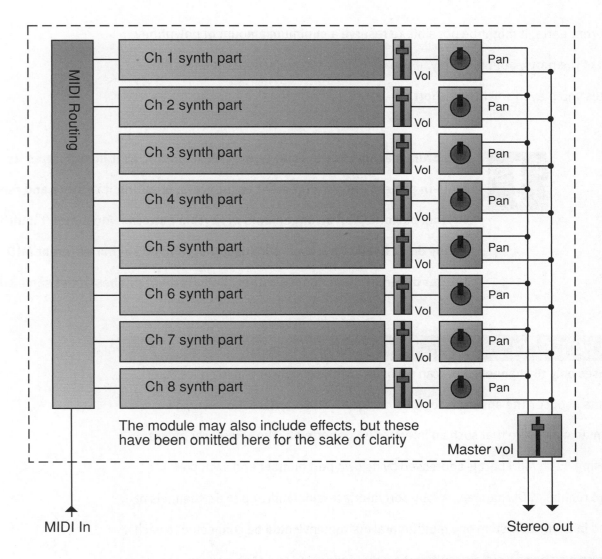

The module may also include effects, but these have been omitted here for the sake of clarity

MIDI In

Stereo out

Figure 2.4: Schematic representation of a multitimbral synth module

internally. However, you can invariably control the relative levels of the different voices, their left/right pan positions and the amount of effect (where available) added to each part. Unfortunately, there is another limitation in that the maximum number of notes that can be played at once (ie the *polyphony*) is shared between all

the different parts. It might be possible to reserve a minimum amount of polyphony for each of the parts, but ultimately, if you try to play too many notes at once, the first notes you played will be cut short.

 The drum machine is a special type of MIDI module as it incorporates its own built-in pattern and arrangement sequencers, enabling it to store and replay rhythm patterns and arrangements of rhythm patterns. Most aren't multitimbral – they don't need to be; their sounds are organised so that different MIDI notes trigger different drum sounds rather than different pitches of the same sound.

MIDI PORTS

If MIDI uses only 16 channels, how can we have a MIDI sequencer playing back 64 or more parts at once? The answer is to use a multiport MIDI interface. However, it's important to make sure that such an interface is supported by the sequencer program you're using. Each MIDI port is addressed by its own port number and each port carries 16 regular MIDI channels. A four-port interface can handle up to 64 channels of MIDI, and in a typical system one multitimbral instrument would be connected to each port. Figure 2.5 shows a simple multiport system connected to a MIDI sequencer.

PROGRAMS AND PATCHES

To recap, you now know how MIDI note data is sent and how the channel system makes it possible to send specific MIDI messages to specific sound modules or other MIDI devices. However, there's a lot more useful information that can be sent via MIDI.

MIDI

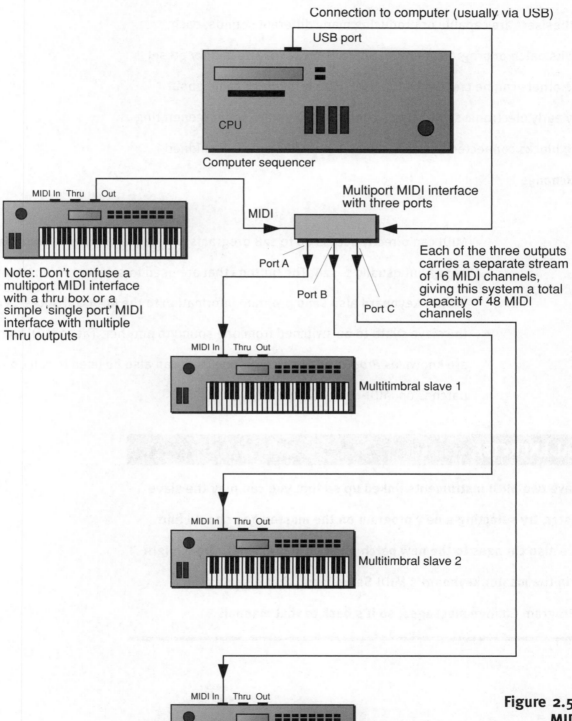

Connection to computer (usually via USB)

USB port

CPU

Computer sequencer

MIDI In   Thru   Out

Note: Don't confuse a
multiport MIDI interface
with a thru box or a
simple 'single port' MIDI
interface with multiple
Thru outputs

MIDI

Multiport MIDI interface
with three ports

Port A

Port B

Port C

Each of the three outputs
carries a separate stream
of 16 MIDI channels,
giving this system a total
capacity of 48 MIDI
channels

MIDI In   Thru Out

Multitimbral slave 1

MIDI In   Thru Out

Multitimbral slave 2

MIDI In   Thru Out

Multitimbral slave 3

**Figure 2.5: Multiport
MIDI interface
connected to a
sequencer**

MIDI

Modern synthesisers are capable or producing many different sounds, each identified by its patch or program number. Some of these may be factory preset sounds while others can be created by the user. (The term *patch* came about because very early electronic synthesisers comprised separate sound-generating or -modifying blocks connected by patch cables, rather like an old-fashioned telephone exchange.)

MIDI can directly access up to 128 programs, which are numbered sometimes 0–127 but usually 1–128. The buttons that are used to select programs on the master keyboard also send program information to the MIDI Out socket, enabling the slave synth to be switched from one sound to another. These MIDI commands are known as *Program Change messages* and can also be used to call up effects patches on MIDI-compatible effects units.

PRACTICAL EXERCISE

If you still have two MIDI instruments linked up so that you can play the slave from the master, try selecting a new program on the master. You should find that the slave also changes to the new patch number. If it doesn't, there might be a facility in the master keyboard's MIDI Setup menu that disables the sending of Program Change messages, so it's back to that manual!

MIDI BANKS

Instruments capable of storing in excess of 128

programs need to have these organised into two or

more banks, each containing a maximum of 128

patches. Bank Select commands – comprising

specific MIDI controller data messages – are then

THE PROS SAY...

Can't hear anything? Is the MIDI cable
plugged in properly?

used to switch from one bank to the next. I could say that these messages are

usually two-part packets of data sent via MIDI controllers 0 and 32, but if this

makes no sense to you at the moment, don't worry – I'll explain what it means

later. Unfortunately, not all MIDI instruments use the same Bank Select messages,

but most modern sequencers can generate Bank Select messages to suit most

common MIDI instruments. To pick a specific sound, you first need to send a Bank

Change command to locate the bank in which the sound is stored and then send a

Program Change message to select the required sound within that bank.

 Some studio effects units are MIDI controllable, where MIDI Program Change messages can be used to call up specific effects from within a library of different effects patches.

MIDI

 WEEK 2 TEST

Week 2's test contains some questions designed to gauge what you've learned about MIDI connections. All the answers are in the preceding week's text.

1   How is MIDI data tagged so that only the intended receiving device responds to it?

2   How many MIDI channels are there?

3   What term is applied to a MIDI instrument capable of playing multiple different parts on different MIDI channels?

4   How can you select a different sound within a MIDI instrument using MIDI?

5   How can you sequence more than 16 channels of MIDI once?

WEEK 3

MIDI CONTROLLERS

So far you've learned that MIDI can be used to send note information from one MIDI device to another and also to select sounds (programs and banks) on a receiving instrument. However, music needs more than note and velocity information to be truly expressive. For example, a violin player might add vibrato to a note or slide from one note to another, and so MIDI must include a number of control functions that will allow the keyboard player to emulate the expression of a real instrument. This section might be the most confusing part of this book to a beginner, but don't let it worry you too much as you can get by with a general overview of what MIDI controllers do. You certainly don't need to memorise them all! As with any unfamiliar technology, you can gain a lot of reassurance just from being told the reason why the various facilities exist.

THE PROS SAY...

You don't need to learn everything; you just need to be aware that it exists.

Most MIDI synthesisers and master keyboards have two or more performance wheels mounted to the left of the keyboard, one of which is usually dedicated to pitch bending and the other to adjusting the depth of modulation. The control information generated by adjusting these wheels can also be sent over MIDI; simply move the control wheel on the master and the slave will respond.

Further control can be provided by means of a footswitch for controlling sustain, or by a volume pedal. A sustain pedal prevents the instrument's note envelopes from entering their release phase until the pedal is released, rather like the

MIDI

sustain pedal on a piano. Because knobs and wheels can be set to any position rather than simply being on or off, they are known as *continuous controllers*. However, because MIDI was conceived to handle numbers in the range 0–127, all continuous controllers really operate over a series of tiny steps rather than being truly continuous. Other physical controls that can send out MIDI data include joysticks, levers, sliders, breath controllers, ribbon controllers, volume pedals and so on. Some controllers have dedicated functions while others can be reassigned so that they control features of specific instruments.

PITCH-BEND SCALING

The extent to which instruments respond to MIDI data can sometimes be determined by the user. For example, the maximum travel of the pitch-bend wheel might be set to cause a pitch shift of as little as one semitone or as much as a whole octave. To avoid confusion, it's usually safest to ensure that all instruments in your system are set up with the same pitch-bend ranges (most users seem to prefer a range of plus/minus two semitones). Be aware, however, that although the pitch-bend wheel is involved in expression control, it doesn't form a part of the mainstream MIDI controllers group; it has a category all of its own.

PRACTICAL EXERCISE

If your master keyboard also produces sounds – for example, if it's a keyboard synthesiser – set it up to control a slave instrument and set the pitch-bend ranges on the master and slave to different amounts. Arrange it so that you can hear both instruments playing at the same time. Now use the pitch-bend wheel

on the master keyboard and listen to the result. The further you move the wheel, the more the pitch of the two keyboards will move out of tune with each other. Now set them to the same value (two semitones is a safe bet) and repeat the exercise. The two pitches should move together. This demonstrates why it's a good idea to have them set to the same value!

MIDI VOLUME

Where master volume is supported via MIDI, turning up the master-volume slider on a controlling device will send the appropriate control information (controller 7) and the receiving synth will respond to it. Note that a multitimbral module receiving a master-volume control message will vary the volume of only that part which corresponds to the MIDI channel of the message.

PRACTICAL EXERCISE

Move the master-volume control on your master keyboard and see if the volume of your slave synthesiser responds. If it does, you know that both master and slave are equipped to deal with MIDI master-volume control.

MORE MIDI CONTROLLERS

Most of the time – at least while you're getting to know MIDI – you'll be concerned mainly with selecting and playing sounds, using the performance wheels on the master keyboard and possibly using a sustain pedal plugged into the back of the master keyboard. However, if you want to try something more sophisticated, you'll be pleased to know that there are 128 possible MIDI controllers in the MIDI

specification. OK, this might be bit advanced for a Crash Course, but if you read
through this section now just to get a feel for what's going on, you can refer back
to it when you get more adventurous.

Of the 128 available MIDI controllers, 0–63 are used for continuous controllers
while 64–95 are used for switches. Continuous controllers are for adjusting things
normally controlled by knobs and faders, where the value can be changed in 128
steps, whereas a switch can simply be either on or off.

MIDI controllers 96–121 are as yet undefined and 122–127 are reserved for
Channel Mode messages. Take a look at the opposite page for a full listing of the
controller numbers and their functions. Not all of these will be familiar, but it
shouldn't be too hard to pick out the common ones, such as volume, pan, bank
select, sustain pedal and so on. Remember that pitch bend isn't part of this list;
it's important enough to warrant its own category.

In the following chart, MSB (Most Significant Bit) and LSB (Least Significant Bit)
are, roughly speaking, computerspeak for coarse and fine adjustments. Both MSBs
and LSBs have a possible numeric range of 0–127, and it sometimes makes sense
to use two controllers to adjust a single function to obtain greater accuracy than
with the basic 128 steps. (By using two controllers, you effectively have 128 x 128,
or 16,384, steps of resolution.) Again, you don't really need to know much about
this; if it proves necessary, your equipment will use it automatically. Controllers 0
and 32 are also usually used to carry Bank Change messages.

CONTROLLER LISTING

0	Bank Select	65	Portamento	94	Celeste Depth (Effect 4)
1	Modulation Wheel	66	Sostenuto	95	Phaser Depth (Effect 5)
2	Breath Controller	67	Soft Pedal	96	Data Increment
3	Undefined	68	Legato Footswitch	97	Data Decrement
4	Foot Controller	69	Hold 2	98	Non-Registered Parameter
5	Portamento Time	70	Sound Variation/Exciter		Number LSB
6	Data Entry	71	Harmonic Content/Compressor	99	Non-Registered Parameter
7	Main Volume	72	Release Time/Distortion		Number MSB
8	Balance	73	Attack Time/Equaliser	100	Registered Parameter Number
9	Undefined	74	Brightness/Expander–Gate		LSB
10	Pan	75	Undefined/Reverb	101	Registered Parameter Number
11	Expression	76	Undefined/Delay		MSB
12	Effect Control 1	77	Undefined/Pitch Transpose	102–119	Undefined
13	Effect Control 2	78	Undefined/Flange–Chorus	120	All Sound Off
14	Undefined	79	Undefined/Special Effect	121	Reset All Controllers
15	Undefined	80–83	General Purpose 5–8	122	Local Control
16–19	General Purpose 1–4	84	Portamento Control	123	All Notes Off
20–31	Undefined	85–90	Undefined	124	Omni Mode Off
32–63	LSB for Control Changes	91	Effects Depth (Effect 1)	125	Omni Mode On
	0–31	92	Tremolo Depth (Effect 2)	126	Mono Mode On
64	Damper/Sustain Pedal	93	Chorus Depth (Effect 3)	127	Poly Mode On

MIDI

 All variable controllers have values ranging from 0–127 (128 steps), while switched controllers are usually set at zero for off and 127 for on. Most modern instruments will also accept any switched-controller value of 64 and above as on and any value below 64 as off. Functions such as pan and pitch bend have a nominal 'centre-neutral' position, with wheel travel being possible in two directions, sending values of 64 when set to neutral.

As you become more familiar with MIDI, you'll discover that you can use a sequencer to automate elements of your performance by controlling levels, pan position, filter settings and so on in real time. Virtually all modern sequencers provide simple visual interfaces that let you view and edit controller data in a graphic manner, allowing you to concentrate on being creative. Don't be intimidated by these MIDI controllers and their meanings, as in most practical applications your sequencer will record and replay whatever MIDI information the master keyboard (or the onscreen controls) sends it without you having to know anything about which controller numbers are involved. If this is the case, you might be asking, why bring the subject up at all? Well, when you're more comfortable with using MIDI sequencers and you find yourself wanting to edit your sequence data, it can be helpful to know what the more common controllers do and what their values represent.

ADVANCED: NON-REGISTERED PARAMETERS

You might never consciously need to use a non-registered parameter, but it helps to know what the term means. No two synthesisers work in exactly the same way, so

it's impossible for the 127 MIDI controllers to access every possible parameter of every instrument. Some criteria – pitch-bend sensitivity, fine tuning, coarse tuning, sustain pedal and so on – are common to all instruments, and these are known as *registered parameters*, but in order to allow manufacturers to provide MIDI access to all the relevant parameters of their specific instruments, the NRPN (Non-Registered Parameter Number) system was incorporated into the MIDI specification.

In fact, the majority of controls on a typical instrument are non-registered, but the day-to-day MIDI user doesn't need to deal with them directly as they exist mainly so that software writers can create editing software that communicates via MIDI. Think of them as a back door into the hidden parameters of an instrument.

PRACTICAL EXERCISE

Familiarise yourself with the actions of pitch bend and other common MIDI controllers. If you have a sequencer connected to your system, operate the various controllers and then look at the data in the sequencer's MIDI Event list. Compare it with the data in the previous table.

THE PROS SAY...

MIDI is just the electrical equivalent of a music score.

MIDI

Another week, another test. This one's designed to find out exactly how much you've picked up on the topic of MIDI controllers over the past week. If you come across any blind spots, you know what to do...

1 What are the two main types of MIDI controller message?

2 What's the numeric range of a continuous controller?

3 Which 'MIDI controller' isn't part of the MIDI controller set?

4 Why were non-registered MIDI parameters (NRPNs) created?

WEEK 4

ASSIGNABLE CONTROLS

Now it's time to dig a little deeper into the control aspects of MIDI. The concept of assignable controls might be a little more advanced than you'll want to deal with right away, but it can be useful if you need to use a control surface of some kind to make real-time changes to your sound using knobs and faders. In this section I'll also introduce some of the more obscure but nevertheless useful aspects of MIDI. Once you've skimmed through it, you can always come back to it later.

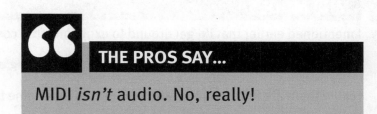

THE PROS SAY...

MIDI *isn't* audio. No, really!

MIDI is all about performance control, and most MIDI keyboard instruments or master keyboards allow you to match up physical control devices to specific MIDI controller numbers. For example, the modulation wheel on your synth could be used to control effect level or filter brightness rather than the usual depth of vibrato. Similarly, you might choose to use a fader or joystick to control portamento (glide) rate or vibrato speed. This assignment is carried out in the MIDI Setup menu of the controlling device, and here you can usually select from a list of available controller functions to determine which type of message a specific physical control will send. Keyboards or stand-alone devices with multiple assignable controls are useful in this respect, not only for real-time performance control but also for controlling MIDI sequencers – for example, a set of MIDI faders could be used to control the playback levels of several MIDI-instrument tracks, just as you could with a regular mixer.

MIDI

MIDI MODES

I mentioned earlier that I'd get around to explaining the concept of MIDI modes, so here goes. We often think of MIDI instruments as working only in one way, but in reality there are four common MIDI modes that determine how an instrument responds to incoming MIDI messages. One of these – Poly mode – is used for almost everything, while the other three are used for more specialised applications.

- **Mode 1: Omni On/Poly** – In this mode, the instrument will play polyphonically but MIDI channel data is ignored. It will play whatever you send to it, regardless of the channel on which it's sent. Mostly, this is not what you want! However, it pretty much guarantees that you'll get a sound out of the instrument, no matter what MIDI note data you send it. Most instruments support this mode, which is commonly referred to simply as 'Omni'.

- **Mode 2: Omni On/Mono** – The monophonic equivalent of mode 1. This mode is hardly ever used and many instruments don't even support it. In this mode, the instrument will attempt to play everything, but only monophonically! In fact, few people can even remember why it was added to the MIDI specification in the first place – and I'm not one of them!

- **Mode 3: Omni Off/Poly** – This is the 'normal' MIDI mode, used especially for sequencing or multitimbral operation. In mode 3, the instrument responds to messages on its own MIDI channel only and plays polyphonically. It's commonly known as 'Poly mode'.

- **Mode 4: Omni Off/Mono** – The monophonic equivalent of mode 3. Mode 4 is mainly for MIDI guitar players who need to have each string working on a separate MIDI channel in order to be able to bend notes or apply vibrato on independent strings. Because each string of a guitar is mono (ie it can play only one note at a time), it makes sense to use the receiving synth in Mono mode in order to emulate the way in which a real guitar plays. This mode may also be used to emulate the way in which analogue monophonic keyboard synths behave and is popular for creating synth bass lines.

 Many synths describe MIDI mode 3 simply as 'Poly mode'. On modern instruments you shouldn't even need to think about it, as they should already be set to Poly mode, but if you have an old MIDI instrument you need to know how to switch modes (via the MIDI Setup menu again), especially if it's one of those annoying instruments that defaults to in Omni mode every time you power it up.

PRACTICAL EXERCISE

Switch your polyphonic slave synth to Poly mode (if it isn't already in that mode), make sure the instrument is sending and receiving MIDI on the same channel and play the master keyboard normally. You'll find that you can play chords as well as melodies. Now try the same thing in Mono mode – whenever you play a new note, the old one stops playing. If you try to play a chord, only the key you pressed last will sound.

MIDI

TOP TIP

Where you have the option to change the polyphony of the slave instrument to get a monosynth effect, set its polyphony to 1 and leave it in Poly mode.

ADVANCED: ACTIVE SENSING

The MIDI specification includes a self-checking feature – totally invisible to the user, although by no means universally implemented – called *active sensing*. This is MIDI's way of checking that a connection exists between devices so that, if the connection is broken, the receiving device can stop sounding. Without active sensing, a connection broken between a Note On and a Note Off message will result in the note being left stuck on.

PRACTICAL EXERCISE

To check whether or not your master and slave instruments have active sensing, unplug the MIDI cable while holding down a MIDI note on the master keyboard and then note whether the slave stops playing or carries on. If it stops playing, you have active sensing. In my experience, however, most instruments will simply keep on droning – hence the need for the next subject...

THE PANIC BUTTON

Most sequencers and many MIDI interfaces have a panic button. This doesn't summon a SWAT team but simply sends MIDI Note Off messages to all notes on all MIDI channels (and all MIDI ports, if there's more than one) to kill stuck notes.

CHANNEL VOICE MESSAGES

The MIDI messages we've focused on so far have all been channel specific, which means that they're acknowledged by the receiving instrument only if they're set to the same channel as that on which the MIDI note data is being sent. MIDI Program Change and Note On and Off messages, as well as velocity, pitch-bend, controller and aftertouch data, all consist of channel messages.

AFTERTOUCH

Channel aftertouch is a common performance control built into many keyboard instruments. It works via a long pressure sensor beneath the keyboard that is used to generate MIDI data in response to pressure on the keys. You can use aftertouch to control such things as volume and vibrato depth by pushing down on the keys as you play, but it's best to switch it off if you're not using it in order to avoid burdening the MIDI data stream with unnecessary data. Aftertouch is a channel message.

 Channel aftertouch affects all notes currently playing, not just the one you're pressing down on, as there's only one sensor covering the entire keyboard. More sophisticated instruments offer *polyphonic aftertouch*, where the MIDI data sent is specific to the key being pressed, but this generates a huge amount of MIDI data and such keyboards are expensive as each key needs its own pressure sensor.

Be aware that the effect generated by aftertouch depends on what is assigned to it. For example, a synth may allow you to use aftertouch to control vibrato depth in one patch and brightness in another.

MIDI

PRACTICAL EXERCISE

Explore the aftertouch capability of your instrument by trying to control different things with it. Adding vibrato by pressing on the keys after playing a note is a useful way of adding musical expression, but also try assigning aftertouch to filter frequency, which will allow you to brighten a sound by pressing harder. Assigning it to loudness can be very effective when playing string parts.

RELEASE VELOCITY

All velocity-sensitive instruments generate MIDI note velocity data, which varies depending on how hard you play, but on instruments that support *release velocity*, additional information is generated depending on how quickly you release the keys. Again, these instruments are fairly specialised and they generate a lot of MIDI data.

SOUNDS IN THE BANK

All conventional MIDI messages have a maximum of 128 steps (usually numbered 0–127), so MIDI can deal with a maximum of 128 different notes or send controller information with a maximum of 128 discrete values. Similarly, you can directly address only 128 different patches. To get around this limitation, though, most synths have sounds organised in multiple banks, with a maximum of 128 patches per bank. MIDI Bank Select messages (special controller messages, often involving controllers 0 and 32) are used to switch between the different banks. While MIDI is all about standardisation, the bank-selecting element was added later on during its evolution, so Bank Select messages don't always take the same form for the

various models of instrument. Check the MIDI implementation chart at the back of your instrument manual to find out what kind of Bank Change message your synth or module expects.

To save the user from getting bogged down with trying to find the right type of Bank Select message for their particular instrument, many software-sequencer developers include libraries of Bank Select commands for all the common instruments in their programs. You just need to tell your sequencer what type of instrument it's connected to and it will find the appropriate Bank Select message for you.

Note that some early instruments, such as the E-mu Proteus, had multiple sound banks but didn't respond to MIDI Bank Change messages. This meant that the banks had to be changed manually, via their front-panel controls.

PRACTICAL EXERCISE

Connect a MIDI instrument that has two or more sound banks to your MIDI sequencer and send it a Bank Select messages to switch to another bank. Confirm that this is happening by watching the display on the receiving instrument as you send the message. Remember that Bank Select messages are channel specific, so if you have a multitimbral instrument, make sure you're monitoring the part that has the same MIDI channel as the messages you're sending. Once you've confirmed that bank selection is taking place, send Program Change messages to check that the patches within the bank are being selected correctly. If this doesn't work, most likely the sending device has a

MIDI

MIDI filter set up to remove certain types of MIDI message, including Bank

Select, or you've sent the wrong type of Bank Select message.

Some of the stuff touched upon in this section is admittedly a little sophisticated for a Crash Course, but a little background information is always useful, even if you choose to stick to the basics for a while. You'll hopefully have tried the various exercises along the way, so all that remains now is to answer a few questions to make sure you've absorbed what you've read...

WEEK 4 TEST

Congratulations – you've made it to the end of Week 4. Now it's time to test you on what you've learnt over the past few days. You should complete this test before moving on to the next section. Good luck!

1   How are MIDI programs arranged when there are more than 128 of them?

2   Which MIDI mode is the 'normal' mode for sequencing and day-to-day use?

3   What system is used to generate MIDI controller data as the performer presses down on the keys of a keyboard?

4   What is a MIDI panic button for?

WEEK 5

MIDI AND TIMING

MIDI includes a special set of messages that look
after synchronisation and sequencer control. These
special messages have no MIDI channel addresses;
they are intended to be received by all the devices in
the MIDI system, and so tend to be known as *system
messages*. Think of them as circular mail that
everyone gets, as opposed to addressed mail.
Perhaps the most important of all these messages is MIDI clock.

THE PROS SAY...

A multitimbral MIDI instrument plus a
sequencer is your orchestra. You are
the composer.

 **Even though every device gets system messages, not all devices are designed to
respond to them or, indeed, need to respond to them.**

MIDI CLOCK

MIDI clock can be thought of as a metronome pulse hidden amongst the other MIDI
data that keeps your drum machine and sequencer playing in time with each other
rather than running at different speeds. MIDI clock is acted upon by any drum
machine or sequencer set to External MIDI Sync mode, enabling the slave machine
to stay synchronised with the master. Some synths may also have a facility that
allows arpeggiators, delays or rhythmic modulations to be locked to MIDI clock.

The simplest use of MIDI clock is to 'sync up' a drum machine to a sequencer,
where either one can be the master. The master machine generates the clock,
and therefore sets the tempo, while the slave machine (set to External MIDI Sync

mode) follows that tempo by locking to the MIDI clock signal being generated by the master.

 The slave machine must always be set to External MIDI Sync or the incoming MIDI clock data will be ignored. Synthesisers without tempo-related functions (such as arpeggiators) will ignore MIDI clock altogether. The master machine is always set to Internal Sync and to output MIDI clock.

PRACTICAL EXERCISE

Connect a drum machine to the MIDI Out of your sequencer, make sure that it's in External MIDI Sync mode and check that it runs in time with the sequencer. If it doesn't start when you start the sequencer, check that it's set to respond to MIDI Start, Stop and Continue commands (see below). These options are usually to be found in – you've guessed it – the machine's MIDI Setup menu.

START, STOP AND CONTINUE

A slave device needs to know when to start and stop, which is why MIDI's repertoire of hidden messages also includes Start, Stop and Continue commands. Although these messages can be used to start and stop the slave device, a slave locked only to MIDI clock has no way of knowing whereabouts in the song the master started playing, so the two machines might run at the same tempo and yet play different parts of the song.

To get around this limitation, MIDI SPP (Song Position Pointer) messages were added to the MIDI specification. Like the Start, Stop and Continue commands, these messages are invisible and inaudible to the user, but they do the important job of telling the slave device whereabouts in the song the master machine was when Play was pressed. As long as both master and slave machines support SPPs, the matching up of time locations will look after itself without a second thought from the user. Some early MIDI sequencers and drum machines didn't support SPPs and so all synchronised playback had to be started from the beginnings of songs. Figure 5.1 shows a drum machine synchronised to a hardware MIDI sequencer.

ADVANCED: SMPTE AND MTC

If you're not using a sequencer, you can skip this section and the next, but if you are and you want to sync it to a tape machine or digital recorder, you might find the next bit useful. The majority of modern sequencers offer MTC (MIDI Time Code) for synchronisation as an alternative to MIDI clock (although they all support MIDI clock as well). MTC is based on the SMPTE (pronounced 'simptee') synchronisation system, originally developed for film and TV work.

SMPTE has nothing to do with MIDI and is a system that transmits real-time information, rather than bars and beats (tempo), over a separate sync cable. SMPTE data deals with hours, minutes, seconds and film/TV frames up to a maximum of 24 hours. For example, the SMPTE readout for 1 hour, 10 minutes, 30 seconds and 11 frames would look like this: '01:10:30:11'. You might have seen these numbers whizzing around on some video-editing systems.

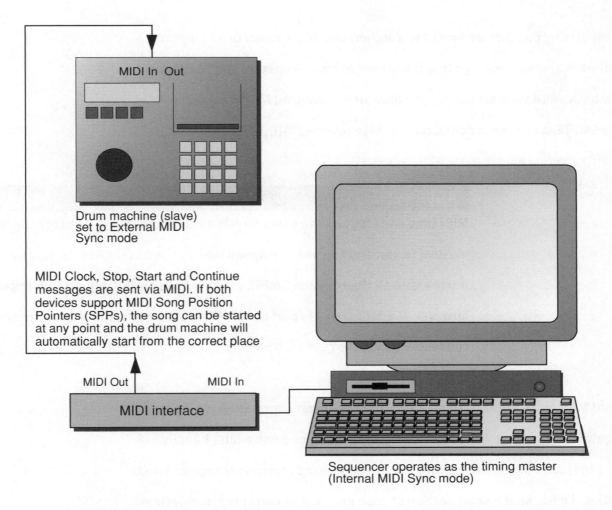

MIDI In Out

Drum machine (slave)
set to External MIDI
Sync mode

MIDI Clock, Stop, Start and Continue
messages are sent via MIDI. If both
devices support MIDI Song Position
Pointers (SPPs), the song can be started
at any point and the drum machine will
automatically start from the correct place

MIDI Out   MIDI In

MIDI interface

Sequencer operates as the timing master
(Internal MIDI Sync mode)

**Figure 5.1: Drum machine synchronised to a
hardware MIDI sequencer**

Because of the different film and TV frame rates used around the world, SMPTE

comes in several frame formats, the most common being 30fps for US TV, 25fps for

European TV and 24fps for film. The term 'SMPTE/EBU' covers all the US and

European formats, but most users stick with the term 'SMPTE' to cover all the

SMPTE/EBU variations. There's also a format called *drop-frame*, which is used

when converting one picture format to another, but this is rarely used for purely musical work and so I won't go into it any further here. As a rule, SMPTE is not used in basic MIDI systems (although some more advanced MIDI interfaces include SMPTE sync connections), but its close relative, MTC, is.

ADVANCED: MTC

MIDI time code follows the same format as SMPTE in that it is independent of musical tempo and expresses elapsed time in hours, minutes, seconds and frames, and all the common SMPTE variants have an MTC equivalent. Importantly, however, the MTC signal is part of the MIDI data stream, not a separate sync connection, as is the case with SMPTE.

Standard MIDI clock sync doesn't include any positional information, so if a sync pulse gets lost, the slave MIDI device will follow along one pulse late, happily unaware that anything is wrong. MTC, on the other hand, comprises regular bursts of positional data, so if a short section of code gets lost or corrupted, the system knows exactly where it's supposed to be the next time a piece of valid code is read. It takes eight 'quarter frame' messages to carry enough data to make up one complete set of location data, which means that the receiving MIDI device must read at least two frames of code before it knows where it's supposed to be. In practical terms, this takes less than a tenth of a second.

Most digital hardware recorders can output MTC directly, which means that a sequencer can be sync'ed to the recorder using no additional hardware other

than a MIDI cable, and normally the recorder is the master and the sequencer the slave. However, as music works in bars and beats rather than pure time, sequencers need to calculate an internal tempo map that converts MTC to tempo, including any tempo changes that the user has programmed into a song. At one time this made the user's job more difficult, but modern sequencers invariably look after the tempo mapping automatically. However, you should be aware that the time-to-tempo calculation involves the rounding up or down of numbers, and so two pieces of gear from different manufacturers fed from the same MTC source and set to run at the same tempo can still drift out of sync with each other slightly over a period of time, depending on how accurately the conversion calculations are handled. MIDI SPPs are not relevant when using MTC as a sync system, as MTC includes its own time-location information; they are needed only for synchronisation via MIDI clock.

 It's safest not to start songs at an MTC time of 00:00:00:00. Instead, it's best to enter an offset (an hour is a convenient amount). This means that the song doesn't play through 'midnight', where 24:00:00:00 changes to 00:00:00:00 during the count-in, which can cause some equipment to behave erratically.

MIDI MACHINE CONTROL

Yet another part of the MIDI protocol was added to allow the remote MIDI controlling of compatible tape machines, hard-disk recorders and so on. MMC (MIDI Machine Control) provides remote MIDI access to the main transport

controls and Record Ready button of a multitrack recorder, allowing the user to control everything from the sequencer.

MIDI LIMITATIONS

While you can control a complete multipart musical performance over a single MIDI cable, MIDI is actually based on a rather outdated serial data system, which means that the MIDI messages follow each other in single file. Knowing about the bits and bytes that make up a MIDI message doesn't really help the typical user to make better use of MIDI, and indeed serves only to confuse the newcomer, so I won't burden you with it here. It's enough to know that each individual MIDI message is very short, so the fact that two notes can't start to sound at exactly the same time isn't obvious, but it you tried to play 100 notes at exactly the same time, you'd hear the 100th note play a little while after the first!

The speed of MIDI is seldom a limitation when you're dealing with only notes, but if you're trying to replay a multipart MIDI sequence that also contains lots of controller information, you could end up with MIDI gridlock. This is why it is important that your sequencer gives timing priority to note events (which, thankfully, most do). To ease the MIDI burden, use controllers only when necessary and turn off your master keyboard's aftertouch facility when you're not using it.

SLIGHTLY MORE OBSCURE...

When MIDI was first introduced, just being able to send notes and Patch Change messages over it was considered to be pretty miraculous, but as with most good

ideas it got revised and new features were bolted onto it as required. In fact, you might be surprised at just what's buried in the current MIDI protocol. Here are just a couple of features you might find useful.

MIDI Song Select

Because some MIDI sequencers can hold more than one song in memory, MIDI also includes a Song Select message. As you might expect with these messages, tunes can be requested by number in the range 0–127, allowing your sequencer to operate as a kind MIDI jukebox that accepts requests via MIDI Song Select numbers!

MIDI Tune Command

While digital MIDI instruments always remain perfectly in tune, MIDI-controlled analogue synths can and will drift in pitch over a period of time unless they have auto-tuning routines built into them. Where they do, the internal tuning routine can be initiated via a message known as a MIDI Tune Request command. When a Tune Request command is sent, all the MIDI instruments in the system that support Tune Request messages will run their tuning routines. Obviously, this isn't something you'd want to do in the middle of a song!

ADVANCED: SYSTEM-EXCLUSIVE MESSAGES

MIDI System Exclusive messages are pretty scary things and get pretty close to anorak territory, although you still need to know what people mean when they talk about System Exclusive (or Sysex for short) messages.

MIDI

Whereas most of MIDI is pretty precisely defined, the system-exclusive facility is provided so that manufacturers can build instruments with different facilities yet still conform to the MIDI specification. For example, an FM synth has different types of controls from an analogue synth or a drum machine, and the standard MIDI protocol can't cover all possibilities. These non-standard facilities might be needed to allow user control via editing software, and also to allow the settings of a machine to be backed up to a computer via MIDI for safe storage. There's a certain similarity of purpose between Sysex messages and the NRPNs discussed earlier, which are used to access certain unique parameters via MIDI controllers.

Rather than use the MIDI channel system for communication, Sysex messages contain an identification code unique to the type of instrument for which they are intended. Where two or more identical instruments are being used in the same system, it's often possible to assign an additional ID number of between 1 and 16 to each one so that no two have exactly the same ID. If they did, they'd all respond to the same Sysex data.

WHAT'S A SYSEX DUMP?

While usually only people who use MIDI to an advanced degree have more than a passing association with the complexities of MIDI Sysex messages, anyone can use them at a basic level for copying patches or banks of patches from a synth into a MIDI storage device – such as a sequencer or MIDI data filer – or vice versa. Here's how.

Almost all MIDI devices have a Sysex dump facility tucked away in their MIDI-configuration pages somewhere – all you have to do is connect the MIDI Out of the

instrument to your sequencer's input, put the sequencer into Record and then start the dump procedure. On some instruments, you can even choose to dump individual banks or effects settings. Sysex data looks like nonsense in your sequencer's Edit list, but it actually holds all of the settings for the patches and effects that have been dumped. You can re-install this dump at a later date to restore the sounds you've saved by playing it back into the MIDI In of the relevant instrument.

TOP TIP

If you're planning to send a piece of MIDI equipment away for servicing, perform a Sysex dump of all its contents before you do so, just in case the machine's memory gets wiped during the process.

Sysex dump data usually takes several seconds to record, after which it can be played back into the instrument at any time and the patches you saved will be restored. In most cases, you can simply play the Sysex data into the instrument to which you wish to transfer the programs, but some instruments might require you to switch them into a receiving mode first.

PRACTICAL EXERCISE

As a quick exercise, try making a Sysex dump from one of your MIDI instruments (you need to connect its MIDI Out to your sequencer's MIDI In for this) and look at the data in your Event Edit list. If you can't see anything, there might be a view filter setting activated that hides Sysex data, so turn this off. If the data records

MIDI

OK, save the song data so that you can use it to restore your synth settings in case the internal battery fails or the instrument needs to be serviced.

TOP TIP

Check out music user groups on the internet, as these often provide free synth programs as Sysex dumps that you can download and load into your synth. Don't forget to back up your own sounds first, though, or they'll be wiped when you load the new ones!

Don't quantise the Sysex dump data after recording or it might not play back properly. Also, you might have trouble getting the instrument to load the data if you play it back at a different tempo to that at which it was recorded.

COMPATIBILITY

Most modern MIDI instruments support all the key features, but the MIDI specification doesn't insist that every instrument supports all of them, which is why that boring-looking MIDI table at the back of your instrument's manual can be very useful. If a MIDI message is received by an instrument that's incapable of responding to that particular type of message, the message is ignored.

WEEK 5 TEST

OK, that's probably enough on the subject of MIDI and timing for you to chew over for a while. Take a stab at the next few questions. The usual rule applies: don't press on until you can answer them all.

1 Which MIDI sync system is directly related to the tempo of the master machine?

2 Which MIDI sync system uses the same real-time system (ie that based on hours, minutes, seconds and frames) as the SMPTE system used in film and TV 'sound to picture' work?

3 What is a common use for MIDI System Exclusive messages?

4 Why are Song Position Pointers important when using MIDI clock for synchronisation?

WEEK 6

GENERAL MIDI

Last week's tutorials included some fairly advanced concepts, most of which you can safely skip over until you need them. As a reward for your patience, the stuff in Week 6 is rather more straightforward.

THE PROS SAY...

General MIDI might sound a little 'safe', but at least you know what you're going to get.

You might have noticed that some synths and soundcards have a 'GM' logo on the front. General MIDI was added later to the MIDI standard and was designed to ensure nominal compatibility, sound-wise, between instruments of different makes. It also defines a basic MIDI specification to which each GM-compatible unit must comply. Some GM synths sound noticeably better than others, but if you've created a composition for piano on a GM instrument, you know you're going to get a piano sound when your song's played back on any other GM instrument, not a violin or a tuba!

General MIDI is particularly useful for sequencer users who swap work with other musicians or who use commercial MIDI song files. If both the MIDI file format and the destination instrument conform to the GM specification, all of the parts will play back with the correct types of sounds.

General MIDI is based around a standard set of 128 voices that include pop, classical and electronic sounds, plus a few sound effects, and these standard voices are always stored at specific program-number locations. For example, the first sound in a GM instrument is always a piano.

 General MIDI is supported only by those instruments or soundcards that bear the GM logo. Furthermore, a GM machine might also include some additional non-General MIDI functions.

General MIDI not only dictates which sounds are located at which program numbers but also to which keys (MIDI Note Numbers) the various drum sounds are mapped (and drums are always on MIDI channel 10 in GM machines). GM also specifies the minimum multitimbrality and polyphony of the machine, so that any instrument can play back any GM file without running out of parts or notes.

DO YOU NEED GENERAL MIDI?

When recording a MIDI composition on a sequencer, in addition to note data the sequencer tracks can also record the Bank and Program Change numbers of every sound you want to call up when that track is played back. However, if you play your sequence back on a friend's non-GM MIDI system, you might well find that all the sounds are completely wrong because, whereas your program 1 might have been a piano, his might be a synth pad or a sound effect.

This kind of chaos is difficult to avoid in the non-GM world, where every user has a free choice of where in their instruments' user memory banks to store the sounds they've created, while factory presets provided with non-GM instruments tend to be arranged fairly arbitrarily. For this reason, even if most of your work uses your own unique sounds, it's useful to have at least one GM instrument in your collection so that you can play commercial GM-format MIDI files or sequences recorded by other musicians.

MIDI

MAIN GM SPECIFICATIONS

GM instruments must be able to play back a minimum of 16 parts on 16 MIDI

channels, with a total polyphony of at least 24 notes. A GM instrument can give

you more than 24 notes of polyphony but never less. Percussion parts must be on

MIDI channel 10, where a minimum set of 47 standard sound types – including the

most common drum and Latin percussion sounds – must be provided, all mapped

in accordance with the GM standard.

If you try to play back more notes than the maximum polyphony of the instrument,

something called *note robbing* takes place and previously played notes are cut off

early so that new notes can be played.

All GM instruments must respond to the same set of MIDI controllers, and the default

ranges set for these controller must be standard. Basic features supported include

pitch-bend data and Reset All Controllers messages (which reset all MIDI controllers

to their default values) and All Notes Off messages (which silence any notes currently

playing). GM machines must also respond to pitch bend, velocity and aftertouch.

THE PROS SAY...

Need more than 16 MIDI channels? You
need a multiport MIDI interface.

GM VOICE TABLE

Program Number	Instrument	Program Number	Instrument
1	Acoustic Grand Piano	22	Accordion
2	Bright Acoustic Piano	23	Harmonica
3	Electric Grand Piano	24	Tango Accordion
4	Honky-Tonk Piano	25	Acoustic Guitar (Nylon)
5	Electric Piano 1	26	Acoustic Guitar (Steel)
6	Electric Piano 2	27	Electric Guitar (Jazz)
7	Harpsichord	28	Electric Guitar (Clean)
8	Clavi	29	Electric Guitar (Muted)
9	Celesta	30	Overdriven Guitar
10	Glockenspiel	31	Distortion Guitar
11	Music Box	32	Guitar Harmonics
12	Vibraphone	33	Acoustic Bass
13	Marimba	34	Electric Bass (Finger)
14	Xylophone	35	Electric Bass (Pick)
15	Tubular Bells	36	Fretless Bass
16	Dulcimer	37	Slap Bass 1
17	Drawbar Organ	38	Slap Bass 2
18	Percussive Organ	39	Synth Bass 1
19	Rock Organ	40	Synth Bass 2
20	Church Organ	41	Violin
21	Reed Organ	42	Viola

MIDI

Program Number	Instrument	Program Number	Instrument
43	Cello	65	Soprano Sax
44	Contrabass	66	Alto Sax
45	Tremolo Strings	67	Tenor Sax
46	Pizzicato Strings	68	Baritone Sax
47	Orchestral Harp	69	Oboe
48	Timpani	70	Cor Anglais
49	String Ensemble 1	71	Bassoon
50	String Ensemble 2	72	Clarinet
51	Synth Strings 1	73	Piccolo
52	Synth Strings 2	74	Flute
53	Choir Aahs	75	Recorder
54	Voice Oohs	76	Pan Flute
55	Synth Voice	77	Blown Bottle
56	Orchestra Hit	78	Shakuhachi
57	Trumpet	79	Whistle
58	Trombone	80	Ocarina
59	Tuba	81	Lead 1 (Square)
60	Muted Trumpet	82	Lead 2 (Sawtooth)
61	French Horn	83	Lead 3 (Calliope)
62	Brass Section	84	Lead 4 (Chiff)
63	Synth Brass 1	85	Lead 5 (Charang)
64	Synth Brass 2	86	Lead 6 (Voice)

Program Number	Instrument	Program Number	Instrument
87	Lead 7 (Fifths)	108	Koto
88	Lead 8 (Bass And Lead)	109	Kalimba
89	Pad 1 (New Age)	110	Bagpipe
90	Pad 2 (Warm)	111	Fiddle
91	Pad 3 (Polysynth)	112	Shanai
92	Pad 4 (Choir)	113	Tinkle Bell
93	Pad 5 (Bowed)	114	Agogo
94	Pad 6 (Metallic)	115	Steel Drums
95	Pad 7 (Halo)	116	Woodblock
96	Pad 8 (Sweep)	117	Taiko Drum
97	FX 1 (Rain)	118	Melodic Tom
98	FX 2 (Soundtrack)	119	Synth Drum
99	FX 3 (Crystal)	120	Reverse Cymbal
100	FX 4 (Atmosphere)	121	Guitar Fret Noise
101	FX 5 (Brightness)	122	Breath Noise
102	FX 6 (Goblins)	123	Seashore
103	FX 7 (Echoes)	124	Bird Tweet
104	FX 8 (Sci-Fi)	125	Telephone Ring
105	Sitar	126	Helicopter
106	Banjo	127	Applause
107	Shamisen	128	Gunshot

(Note that some manufacturers number their patches from 0–127 rather than from 1–128.)

MIDI

GM DRUM MAP

MIDI Note Number	Drum Sound	MIDI Note Number	Drum Sound
35	Acoustic Bass Drum	56	Cowbell
36	Bass Drum 1	57	Crash Cymbal 2
37	Side Stick	58	Vibraslap
38	Acoustic Snare	59	Ride Cymbal 2
39	Hand Clap	60	High Bongo
40	Electric Snare	61	Low Bongo
41	Low Floor Tom	62	Mute Hi Conga
42	Closed Hi-Hat	63	Open Hi Conga
43	High Floor Tom	64	Low Conga
44	Pedal Hi-Hat	65	High Timbale
45	Low Tom	66	Low Timbale
46	Open Hi-Hat	67	High Agogo
47	Low Mid Tom	68	Low Agogo
48	High Mid Tom	69	Cabasa
49	Crash Cymbal	70	Maracas
50	High Tom	71	Short Whistle
51	Ride Cymbal 1	72	Long Whistle
52	Chinese Cymbal	73	Short Guiro
53	Ride Bell	74	Long Guiro
54	Tambourine	75	Claves
55	Splash Cymbal	76	High Woodblock

MIDI Note Number	Drum Sound	MIDI Note Number	Drum Sound
77	Low Woodblock	80	Mute Triangle
78	Mute Cuica	81	Open Triangle
79	Open Cuica		

VARIATIONS ON A THEME

Roland have developed an enhanced version of General MIDI called GS, which adds several alternative banks of additional sounds to the basic GM set (Bank 0). These banks of 'variation tones' are arranged in such a way that they have the same Program Change numbers as the tones to which they are related. Meanwhile, Bank Change commands allow the user to switch between the various banks. Conventional Program Change commands are then used to select the sounds within each bank.

Yamaha also have developed their own expanded General MIDI format, which they call XG. Like Roland's GS, this enhances the basic General MIDI sound set with several banks of alternative sounds.

GENERAL MIDI SONG FILES

Commercial GM song files are available for many popular songs, and some are made freely available over the internet. MIDI files can be used by solo performers to provide musical backings, within the conditions imposed by music copyright law.

MIDI

One advantage that a MIDI song file has over a pre-recorded karaoke disc is that the key and/or tempo of a MIDI file can be changed very easily. Furthermore, if you have a little skill with a software MIDI sequencer, you can edit the arrangements in order to lengthen solos, add verses and so on.

Standard Formats

Standards are such a good idea that there are lots of them! In fact, there are actually three different versions of standard MIDI file, known as formats 0, 1 and 2.

- **Format 0** – The entire song is saved as just one sequencer track, which means that some unravelling is needed in order to separate the tracks by MIDI channel number.

- **Format 1** – The tracks are kept separate, but any pattern information is lost, so the whole song is effectively transferred as a single pattern.

- **Format 2** – Similar to format 1, but pattern information is also retained.

Format 1 is the most common type of standard MIDI file, but even with these files you might find that the tracks don't load into your sequencer with their original MIDI channel numbers, and sometimes they lose their names, too, depending on how the sequencer creating the file dealt with standard MIDI files. Restoring the original order is fairly straightforward, provided that you make a note as to which instruments are supposed to be playing on which MIDI channels.

Standard MIDI files cater for up to 16 channels of MIDI data.

PRACTICAL EXERCISE

If you have a General MIDI synth or soundcard, try to get hold of a GM MIDI file and import it into your sequencer. If all goes well, the song should play back with the correct sounds, pan positions and levels.

MIDI

WEEK 6 TEST

With Week 6 under you belt, you should now know
enough about General MIDI to progress to the next
level. Have a crack at the test below to make sure
your knowledge is up to speed.

1   How many standard programs or sounds does General MIDI specify?

2   Which MIDI channel controls the drum sounds in a GM-compatible instrument?

3   Which two manufacturers have created extended versions of the General MIDI
specification?

4   How much polyphony must a General MIDI instrument have?

WEEK 7

SEQUENCING

I've already spoken briefly about what a sequencer
can do, and this week the plan is to get you familiar
with the basics of your sequencing system, which
could be either a hardware machine or one based
around computer software. A detailed examination of

sequencers is beyond the scope of this book, and in any event every sequencer
operates a little differently, so there's no alternative to reading the manual for
each one. For more information on sequencers and MIDI in general, you're best off
reading my book *MIDI For The Technophobe*, also published by SMT.

The first thing to do is connect up your sequencer and MIDI instruments correctly.
Your master keyboard's MIDI Out should be connected to the MIDI In of your MIDI
sequencer, interface or soundcard, and if your keyboard is also a synthesiser and
you want to make use of its internal sounds, select Local Off in its MIDI Setup
menu and plug a second MIDI cable from the sequencer's MIDI Out to the
keyboard's MIDI In. If you have any other MIDI instruments you wish to connect to the system, you can daisy-
chain them by connecting the MIDI Thru of the first instrument to the MIDI In of the
next module along in the chain, although a MIDI thru box is a better option here if
you have more than two or three MIDI instruments. Figure 7.1 over the page shows
a typical MIDI system comprising several modules connected via a multiport MIDI
interface and a MIDI thru box. If you're using virtual instruments – which could be
software synths, samplers or drum machines, for example – as sound sources,
you'll also need a suitable soundcard and audio drivers. Normally the

MIDI

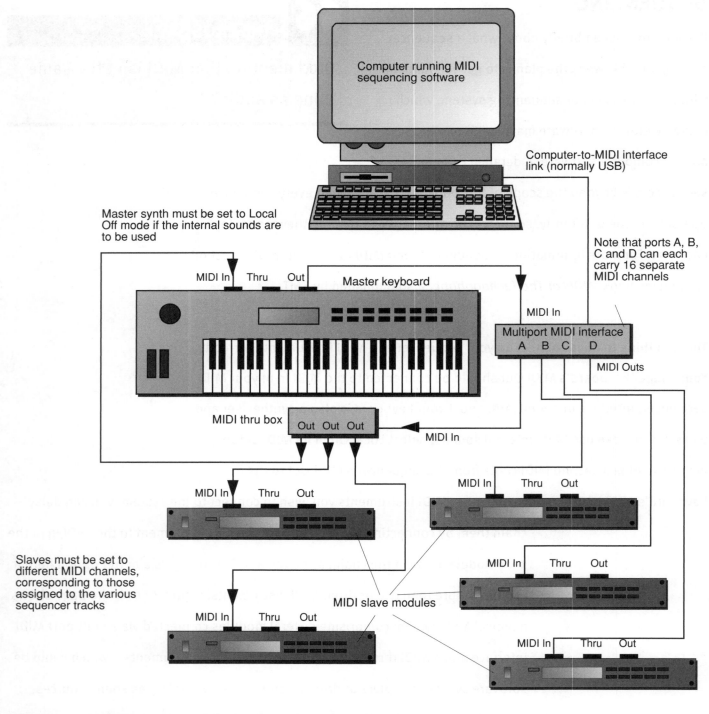

Computer running MIDI sequencing software

Computer-to-MIDI interface link (normally USB)

Master synth must be set to Local Off mode if the internal sounds are to be used

Note that ports A, B, C and D can each carry 16 separate MIDI channels

MIDI In   Thru   Out   Master keyboard

MIDI In

Multiport MIDI interface
A   B   C   D

MIDI Outs

MIDI thru box   Out   Out   Out

MIDI In

MIDI In   Thru   Out

MIDI In   Thru   Out

Slaves must be set to different MIDI channels, corresponding to those assigned to the various sequencer tracks

MIDI In   Thru   Out

MIDI slave modules

MIDI In   Thru   Out

MIDI In   Thru   Out

Figure 7.1: Typical MIDI system comprising several modules connected via a multiport MIDI interface and a MIDI thru box

soundcard's audio outputs would be connected to the same mixer as your hardware audio instruments.

If you're new to computers, you should familiarise yourself with opening and closing programs, saving files and navigating through the various folders before attempting to use your sequencer. And if you're at the stage of buying a computer sequencer package, it's safest to buy it ready configured from a music specialist so that you know you've got a working system. All hardware and software sequencers work slightly differently to each other, so you're going to have to spend some time reading manuals, but if you have a friend who already uses the same system, some guidance in those first few hours can be invaluable.

The rest of this week focuses primarily on the elements of software-based sequencers, although the basic functions of both hardware and software models are similar. As a rule, the desktop-computer-based systems have a more advanced graphical editing environment.

IF MIDI ISN'T AUDIO, WHY DOES MY SEQUENCER HAVE AUDIO TRACKS?

A modern sequencer invariably has both MIDI tracks, which record MIDI music data, and audio tracks, which collectively function more the way in which a regular multitrack tape machine records sound. The MIDI tracks are used to record performances on electronic instruments, providing all the editing benefits that MIDI has to offer, while the audio tracks are used to record vocals, guitars and other

traditional instruments, and you'll need a microphone and either a mixer or mic preamp to record these. Although the audio tracks have little in common with MIDI tracks, they are shown in the same Arrange-page environment, and the same cut/copy/paste editing can be performed on them. MIDI can also be used to control certain aspects of an audio track, such as level or pan position. However, as this book is specifically about MIDI, I shan't be covering sequencer audio in any detail.

THE ARRANGE PAGE

There are fewer than half a dozen major sequencer packages available for desktop computers (mainly Windows PC and Apple Mac) and all tend to follow the same basic operational style, where the main page shows the sequencer tracks running

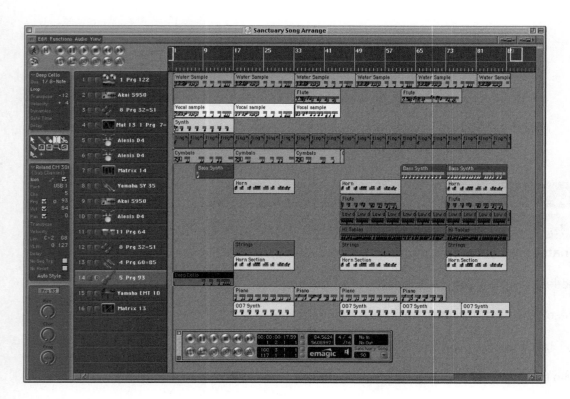

Figure 7.2: Sequencer Arrange page

from left to right across the screen. This main page tends to be known as the Arrange page, and Figure 7.2 provides a typical example.

MIDI performances are recorded into the currently selected track and can include Program Change and Bank Change messages as well as controller and note data. Normally you'll play along to a click track generated by the sequencer, and this can be set to any tempo. Usually, you get a one- or two-bar count-in before recording starts.

On playback, the recorded MIDI data is sent to the MIDI channel to which the track is set, regardless of the channel to which the master keyboard is set (although it's usually safest to leave it set to channel 1), and on most systems MIDI data is also output on this same MIDI channel during recording so that you can hear the slave synth play as you record.

PRACTICAL EXERCISE

Your first task should be to work through those parts of the manual that show you how to record and play back a track of music. It's usually pretty straightforward, but if you have a friend who uses the same system, now might be a good time to invite him or her over for coffee, as a little guidance can go a long way. Once you've mastered recording and playing back a track, move on to a new track and try to add a second part in time with the first. Again, this should be pretty straightforward, and once you've accomplished it you're well on your way to being able to use your sequencer effectively. Of course, there are many other things hidden in those menus, but most of them can wait until you need them.

LEARNING TO EDIT

Once you've recorded something, experiment a little by moving the MIDI data to new positions in the song and by copying and pasting it into your arrangement multiple times. The tools that allow you to do this are usually presented in a tool palette. Firstly, you'll need the scissors tool (or something similar) to divide a part of your recording into separate sections. After you've done this, the key commands for cutting, copying and pasting these sections are usually the same as those used in word processing, while moving the data is usually simply a matter of dragging it around the screen with the mouse. If you cut on the bar lines, the sections you create will still be in time if you copy or move them to other bar locations. Give it a try. It doesn't have to be great music, just something to help you familiarise yourself with these basic editing tools.

Most sequencers also have a facility for merging the data on different tracks into a single track, often using a tool represented by a tube-of-glue icon in the tool palette. This combines all selected tracks into one – useful if you've recorded a drum part in several layers but want to tidy up the screen by combining all the layers into one track.

QUANTISING

If you're a proficient player, your performance will probably sound fine as it is, but if your timing is a little suspect, try out the sequencer's quantise function. This forces every note you've played to move to the nearest quantise measure on an invisible grid that can be set to just about any bar division, from 1 note to 96 notes per bar. If there's a percentage-quantise function in your sequencer, this will help you to tighten up your playing without losing all the 'feel'.

MORE ON EDITING

Now might be a good time to locate your sequencer's transpose function, which usually works on individual tracks or sections of tracks. Use it to move the melody part up or down by an octave. How does that sound? Once you've mastered this, try transposing all the tracks by the same amount and listen to your composition in a completely different key. Make sure you don't transpose your drum tracks, though, or you'll hear the part being played back with all the wrong drum sounds!

THE PROS SAY...

Don't quantise everything or your music will sound mechanical.

GRID EDIT

Now it's time to leave the Arrange page and take a look at the Grid Edit page, sometimes known as the *piano-roll editor*. Most sequencers have one of these Grid Edit pages, where the notes are represented as bars on a grid depicting time (in beats and bars) in one direction and pitch (in semitones) in the other. A piano-keyboard graphic is usually used to depict the note pitches, as shown in the example of a typical Grid Edit page in Figure 7.3. On this page, you can correct wrong notes in either pitch or time by dragging them to new locations in the grid. Try it for yourself. It's a great way of tidying up an imperfect performance.

SCORE EDIT

Traditionally trained musicians usually prefer to edit notes on the stave, and most serious software sequencers have a Score Edit page for this purpose. Here, notes can be physically dragged to new pitches, deleted or inserted, and the more

advanced packages allow you to prepare a reasonably professional-looking

multipart score that can be printed out, if required.

 TOP TIP

Even if you're used to working with traditional notation, it's still worth using the Grid Edit page too as it shows more detail of the actual note positions and, importantly, exactly where those notes finish. Some systems also use colour to indicate the velocity (ie loudness) of each note.

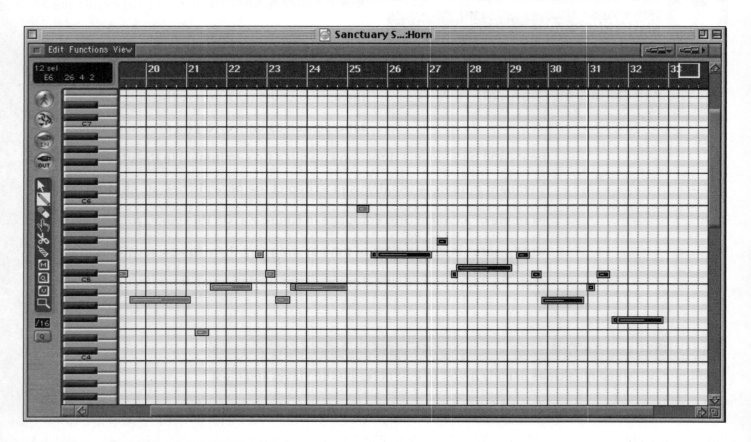

Figure 7.3: Sequencer Grid Edit page

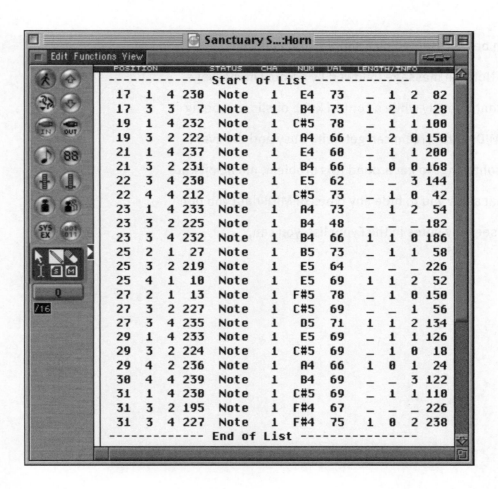

Figure 7.4: Typical sequencer Event list

EVENT LIST

Another popular page is the MIDI Event list, which simply represents the contents

of a selected track as a long list of MIDI events, where each note is marked with its

length and its beat and bar location. Values in this list can be altered by scrolling

to new values or by clicking and entering new values. Try this out for yourself and

refer back to the Grid Edit page to confirm that the note values or timings have

changed. Figure 7.4 shows a typical Event list.

MIDI

Be aware that, while a note can be represented by a simple MIDI message comprising only velocity and a Note On message followed by a Note Off message, controller information is sent continuously while a control knob or slider is being moved, which means that the MIDI data stream can get quite busy and the Event list can end up looking rather confusing. To get around this problem, most software sequencers offer *view filters* that allow you to hide any types of MIDI data you don't want to see. So, if you need to see only notes in the Event list, you can.

WEEK 7 TEST

With Week 7 out of the way, we're nearing the end of this Crash Course. By now you should have a pretty good idea of what MIDI is capable of doing for you. Even so, make sure you can ace the following test before tackling the final week.

1 Why is it necessary to play to a click track if you wish to edit your recorded data?

2 Where would you use quantisation?

3 Which sequencer window allows you to see the notes you've played as a list of note values and timing positions?

4 Why does the Grid Edit page show more musical detail than the Score Edit page?

WEEK 8

SEQUENCING – THE ADVENTURE BEGINS

The previous week only scratched the surface of MIDI sequencing, but if you've

mastered the basic recording and editing skills mentioned so far, you know

enough to start making music on your sequencer.

> Provided that you've understood the concept of MIDI note data, channels and
>
> Program Change messages, plus the rudiments of connecting MIDI systems, you
>
> should have no problem getting started on your creative journey and you can
>
> expand your knowledge in small steps as and when you feel the need. I still flick
>
> through the manual for my sequencer and discover functions I never knew existed,
>
> so keep yours close at hand, and if you find an interesting function you feel might be
>
> useful, make a note of it, along with any key commands or menu locations that will
>
> help you to find it quickly. Then try it out during your next session.

You can wait to explore the more advanced features until you feel you need them, so

a good tip is to skim through the manual just to see what's possible so that, when a

new challenge arises, you'll have an idea of where to look for a solution.

DON'T PANIC!

Modern sequencers combine multitrack audio recording with MIDI sequencing

facilities; they can support software instrument plugins, software effects and

automated mixing. In other words, they include absolutely everything the top

professional studios have at their disposal. With this in mind, don't expect

everything to make sense right away, unless you already know how to use every item

in a professional recording studio! Reading books and music magazines such as the UK's *Sound On Sound* will help you to get up to speed quickly, and there are many useful articles available for free download at www.soundonsound.com that explain many of the basic principles. The secret is always to start with the basics of recording and playback and then progress on to simple editing. Only when you're comfortable doing this should you move on. Most sequencer users develop a way of working that they're happy with, and this might mean using as little as 5% of the available features, so don't feel guilty about not knowing everything – nobody does. All you need to know is enough to stop the technology from getting in the way of your music.

TROUBLESHOOTING

If your system isn't behaving as you think it should, the following checklist might help, but the points here assume that any software you have is already correctly installed. If you don't feel confident about configuring your computer yourself, it's safer to buy a complete system from a music-tech supplier specialising in MIDI sequencing so that you can be confident that the system will work as a whole. If you assemble your own system, problems can arise for the most obscure technical reasons, especially if you're using a PC, in which case you have a huge number of hardware permutations from which to choose.

- If you get no sound, make sure that the sound system into which your MIDI instruments are plugged is switched on and the levels are turned up. Next, check your MIDI cable connections, double-checking that you haven't mistaken a MIDI Out for a MIDI In.

MIDI

- If two or more instruments try to play the same part, the chances are you've either got two or more modules set to the same MIDI channel or one or more instruments are set to Omni mode.

  - If your master keyboard plays its own sounds when you're trying to record with the sound of another module, make sure that Local mode is set to Local Off in the keyboard's MIDI Setup menu.

- If you're plagued with stuck or rapidly repeating notes, you might have a MIDI loop. These are usually caused by Local On being activated when it should be set to Local Off. If you have an older keyboard with no Local Off mode, disable your sequencer's MIDI thru function on whichever channel your master keyboard is transmitting. Check your sequencer manual to find out how to do this.

  - If the sequencer records OK but the wrong sound plays back, you might have forgotten to enter a MIDI Program Change message into your sequencer track. This kind of thing can also happen when you loop (repeat) a section of MIDI data that contains a Program Change command.

WEEK 8 TEST

That's it – you've completed this Crash Course in the basics of MIDI and how to use it. Just to finish things off, here are a few quick questions on the material covered in Week 8. Once you can answer these, you can go off and enjoy yourself. Go on – experiment!

1   What's the most common cause of stuck or mistriggering notes in a MIDI system?

2   In an otherwise correctly set-up MIDI system, what else can cause stuck notes?

3   How can you make sure that your sequencer's MIDI tracks always play back the correct synth patches?

4   What should you check if one of your synths seems to be playing back too many parts at once?

5   If your synth won't respond to MIDI Bank Change messages, what should you check?

GLOSSARY

Active Sensing

Part of the MIDI protocol that involves the master device sending frequent short messages to the receiving slave device to confirm that it is still responding. If the messages stop, the slave will switch off all notes that are currently sounding. Note that most modern instruments do not include this feature.

ADSR

Simple type of envelope generator with attack, sustain, decay and release parameters. ADSRs were first used on early analogue synthesisers and continue to be popular on modern instruments. See *Decay* for more details. Envelopes can also be used to control other synth parameters such as filter-cutoff frequency.

Aftertouch

Means of generating a control signal based on the degree of pressure that is applied to the keys of a MIDI keyboard. Most instruments that support this do not have independent pressure sensing for all keys but instead detect the overall pressure via a sensing strip running beneath the keys. Aftertouch can be used to control such functions as vibrato depth, filter brightness and loudness.

Channel

In MIDI terms, *channel* refers to one of 16 possible data channels over which MIDI data may be sent. The organisation of data by channels means that up to 16 different MIDI instruments or parts may be addressed using a single cable. In the context of mixing consoles, a channel relates to a single strip of controls relating to one input.

Chase

Term used to describe the process whereby a slave device attempts to sync itself with a master device and play from the correct location. In the context of a MIDI sequence, it can also apply to chasing events – looking back to earlier positions in a song to see if there are any Program Change messages or other events that need to be acted upon.

Decay

Progressive reduction in the amplitude of a sound or electrical signal over time. In the context of an ADSR envelope generator, the decay phase starts as soon as the attack phase has reached its maximum level. In the decay phase, the signal level drops until it reaches the sustain level, as determined by the user. The signal then remains at this level until the key is released, at which point the release phase is entered.

Digital

Term used to describe an electronic system in which data and signals are represented in the form of code comprising ones and zeros.

Driver

Piece of software that acts as a link between the host software and a connected piece of hardware, such as a soundcard.

Envelope

Term used to describe the way in which the level of a sound or signal varies over a period of time.

MIDI

Envelope Generator

Circuit capable of generating a control signal representing the envelope of the sound to be recreated. This may then be used to control the level of an oscillator or other sound source, although envelopes can also be used to control filter or modulation settings. The most common example is the ADSR generator.

Event

In MIDI terms, an event is a single unit of MIDI data, such as a note being turned on or off, a piece of controller information or a Program Change message.

File

Meaningful list of data stored in digital form. A standard MIDI file is a specific type of file designed to allow sequence information to be interchanged between different types of sequencer.

Filter

Powerful type of tone-shaping network used in synthesisers to create tonal sweeps and wah-wah effects. The term *filter* can also be applied to some MIDI sequencers which have the provision to exclude, or filter out, certain types of MIDI data, such as aftertouch.

FM

Abbreviation of *frequency modulation*, a type of synthesis whereby one waveform modulates the frequency of another to produce a series of complex harmonics.

General MIDI

Addition to the basic MIDI specification to ensure a minimum level of compatibility when playing back General MIDI-format song files. The GM specification includes such criteria as types and program numbers of sounds, minimum levels of polyphony and multitimbrality and response to controller information.

GM Reset

Universal Sysex command that activates the General MIDI mode on a GM instrument. The same command also sets all controllers to their default values and switches off any notes still playing by means of an All Notes Off message.

Host-powered

Term used to describe software that runs on a computer's own CPU rather than on plugin DSP cards.

Latency

Delay between a note being played on a MIDI keyboard and the sound of a software instrument being produced at the output of the soundcard or interface. Latency can be minimised by using a fast computer and efficient audio drivers, and by setting the minimum audio buffer size that will allow the system to work reliably.

LFO

Abbreviation of *low-frequency oscillator*, a filter used as a modulation source (for example, for vibrato or tremolo), usually below 20Hz. The most common LFO

waveshape is the sine wave, although they often give a choice of sine, square,
triangular and sawtooth waveforms.

Local On/Off
Function that will allow a keyboard and sound-generating section of a keyboard
synthesiser to be used independently of each other.

LSB
Abbreviation of *least significant byte*. If a piece of data has to be conveyed as two
bytes, one byte represents high-value numbers and the other low-value
numbers, much in the same way as tens and units function in the decimal
system. The high value, or most significant part of the message, is called the
MSB (Most Significant Byte).

MIDI
Abbreviation of *musical instrument digital interface*, a system introduced in the
early 1980s to allow music information to be communicated between electronic
instruments and sequencing devices using a standard protocol. MIDI is the
electronic equivalent of a music score. And it is not audio!

MIDI Bank Change
Type of controller message used to select alternate banks of MIDI programs where
access to more than 128 programs is required.

MIDI Control Change

Also known as *MIDI controllers* or *controller data*, these messages convey positional information relating to performance controls such as wheels, pedals and switches. This information can be used to control functions such as vibrato depth, brightness, portamento, effects levels and many other parameters.

MIDI Controller

Interface by means of which a musician plays a MIDI synthesiser or some other kind of sound generator. Examples include keyboards, drum pads and wind synths.

MIDI File

Standard file format for storing song data recorded on a MIDI sequencer in such a way as to enable it to be read by other MIDI sequencers. The three variants of this file format are described in Week 6, 'General MIDI'.

MIDI Implementation Chart

Chart usually found in MIDI product manuals that provides information concerning the MIDI features that are supported. Supported features are marked with a zero while unsupported feature are marked with a cross. Additional information, such as the exact form of Bank Change messages used, may also be provided.

MIDI In

Socket used to receive information from a master controller or from the MIDI Thru socket of a slave unit.

MIDI Merge

Device or sequencer function that enables the combination of two or more streams of MIDI data.

MIDI Mode

MIDI information can be interpreted by the receiving MIDI instrument in a number of ways, the most common being polyphonically on a single MIDI channel (on an instrument set to Poly/Omni Off mode, which enables a MIDI instrument to play all incoming data regardless of channel).

MIDI Module

Sound-generating device with no integral keyboard.

MIDI Note Number

Each key on a MIDI keyboard has its own note number, ranging from 0–127, where 60 represents middle C. Some systems use C3 as middle C while others use C4.

MIDI Note Off

MIDI message sent when a key is released.

MIDI Note On

MIDI message sent when a note is played (ie a key is pressed).

MIDI Out

MIDI connector used to send data from a master device to the MIDI In of a

connected slave device.

MIDI Port

Comprises the MIDI connections of a MIDI-compatible device. A *multiport*, in the

context of a MIDI interface, is a device with multiple MIDI output sockets, each

capable of carrying data relating to a different set of 16 MIDI channels. Multiports

are the only means of exceeding MIDI's limitation of 16 channels.

MIDI Program Change

Type of MIDI message used to change the sound patch on a remote module or the

effects patch on a MIDI effects unit.

MIDI Sync

Describes the synchronisation systems available to MIDI users – MIDI clock and MTC

(MIDI Time Code).

MIDI Thru

On a slave unit, a socket that's used to feed the MIDI In socket of the next unit in line.

MIDI Thru Box

Device that splits the MIDI Out signal of a master instrument or sequencer to remove

the need to daisy-chain devices. Powered circuitry is used to 'buffer' the outputs in

order to avoid running into problems when many pieces of equipment are driven from a single MIDI output.

MMC

Abbreviation of *MIDI machine control*, a system for starting, stopping and pausing a hardware recording device via MIDI. The Record Enable status of individual multitrack recorder tracks may also be set using MMC.

Monitor

Possibly the most used word in recording and, confusingly, one used to describe several different things. For example, observing the status of a process is known as monitoring, so if a synth has a flashing light that indicates MIDI data is being received, this is a form of MIDI monitor. The term *monitoring* also applies to the act of listening to studio loudspeakers, and of course a monitor is also a VDU screen attached to a desktop computer. In live performance, meanwhile, a monitor is an onstage speaker allowing performers to hear themselves and their fellow musicians.

MTC

Abbreviation of *MIDI time code*, a real-time code based on the SMPTE format, used to convey timing information from one device to another.

Multiport MIDI Interface

The MIDI system is limited to carrying 16 channels of information, and to exceed

this it's necessary to run two or more separate streams of MIDI data using what's known as a *multiport MIDI interface*. This can be used only with sequencing software that supports multiple MIDI ports.

Multitimbral Module

MIDI sound source capable of producing several different sounds at once, which can then be controlled on different MIDI channels.

Non-registered Parameter Number

Addition to the basic MIDI specification that allows controllers 98 and 99 to be used to control non-standard parameters relating to particular models of synthesiser. This is an alternative to using system-exclusive data to achieve the same ends, although NRPNs tend to be used mainly by Yamaha and Roland instruments.

Oscillator

Circuit designed to generate a periodic electrical waveform.

Patch

Alternative term for *program*, referring to a single programmed sound within a synthesiser that can be called up using Program Change commands. MIDI effects units and samplers also have patches.

Pitch Bend

Control data specifically designed to produce a change in pitch in response to the

movement of a wheel or lever. Pitch-bend data can be recorded and edited, just like any other MIDI controller data, even though it isn't part of the controller-messages group.

Plugin

Piece of software designed to add capabilities and features to a host application.

Polyphony

Describes the ability of an instrument to play two or more notes simultaneously. An instrument that can play only one note at a time is described as being *monophonic*.

Portamento

Gliding effect whereby a sound changes pitch at a gradual rate, rather than abruptly, when a new key is pressed or a MIDI note is sent.

Pressure

Alternative term for *aftertouch*.

Quantising

Means of moving notes in a MIDI sequencer so that they line up with user-defined subdivisions of a bar of music – for example, 16th notes. It may be used to correct timing errors, although too much can remove the human 'feel' from a performance.

RAM

Abbreviation of *random access memory*. This is a type of memory used by computers

for the temporary storage of programs and data, and all data stored in RAM is lost when the power is turned off. For this reason, work needs to be saved to disk if it is not to be erased.

Release

Rate at which a signal amplitude decays once a key has been released.

Sequencer

Device for recording and replaying MIDI data, usually in a multitrack format, allowing complex compositions to be built up one part at a time.

Sine Wave

Waveform of a pure tone containing no harmonics.

Slave

MIDI device under the control of a master device, such as a sequencer or master keyboard.

SMPTE

Time code used by professionals in the film and TV industries. SMPTE conveys real-time information in hours, minutes, seconds and frames.

Song Position Pointer

Addition to the MIDI protocol that enables devices slaved to MIDI clock to start

MIDI

playing at the correct point within a song if the song is not started from the beginning.

Timbre

The tonal 'colour' of a sound.

Tremolo

Process involving the modulation of a sound's amplitude via a low-frequency oscillator.

Triangle Wave

Symmetrical, triangular wave containing only odd harmonics, but with a lower harmonic content than a square wave.

USB

Abbreviation of *universal serial buss*, a standard interface for connecting peripherals such as scanners, cameras, audio interfaces and MIDI interfaces to both Mac and PC computers. USB is also a commonly used interface for the connection of security keys in an attempt to prevent software piracy.

Velocity

Rate at which a key is depressed. On later synths, velocity data may be used to control loudness (to simulate the response of instruments such as pianos) or other parameters.

Vibrato

Pitch modulation whereby an LFO (Low-Frequency Oscillator) modulates a VCO (Voltage-Controlled Oscillator).

Virtual Instrument

Instrument that runs entirely within software, rather than hardware, form. Virtual instruments are played from MIDI keyboards just like regular hardware instruments, and many also respond to MIDI controller information. Virtual instruments tend to operate as plugins (available in formats such as VST, Direct X, Audio Units, RTAS, MAS and so on) within a host sequencer program or other audio software. The sound from a virtual (VT) instrument comes via the outputs of the soundcard or audio interface attached to the computer.

Voice

Describes the capacity of a synthesiser to play a single musical note. An instrument capable of playing 16 simultaneous notes is said to be a '16-voice' instrument.

VST

Abbreviation of *Virtual Studio Technology*, a system devised by Steinberg to enable plugin instruments and effects to be used within music software packages.

XG

Yamaha's alternative to Roland's GS system for enhancing the General MIDI protocol so as to provide additional banks of patches and further editing facilities.